Kaleidoscope of Being

Jennifer Toth

Olympus Story House

CONTENTS

Dedication

For my Lord and Savior, Jesus Christ, without whom,
I would never have survived 45 years on planet
earth. Jesus Raised me, Carried me, Comforted me,
Taught me, Guided me, Saved me, and
Ultimately, Set Me Free! I will NEVER be able to
repay Him for His Love, which is beyond measure,
nor His time, which He is beyond generous with.
Jesus is my Savior but also my
Best Friend Above All.

John 3:16 "For God so loved the world, that he gave
his only begotten Son, that whosoever believeth
in him should not perish, but have everlasting life".

- KJV

Allow Me to Introduce Myself

I had stars in my sandbox,
I used moonbeams as slides!
I showered in the rain,
Under the sun, I dried!
I ate honey from the hive
Drank fresh dew
Played with the wind and always
Tagged along with some sunbeams I knew!
I understood the language of birds
Sang with them every morn'
I was on fire in my youth,
A real ethereal storm!
But then came the thunder
And the lightening too,
As my days of youth were being spent,
Older and older I grew
I began to forget all that I knew
But the wind does not forget
And still whispers my name,
Wildflower, it speaks
"You are not to blame."

Chatting with Jesus Over Tea

"Ah, to love, to truly love
As I have loved,
Is to be completely free"
God said to me quite cheerfully
As we sat in my garden,
Chatting over tea.
I often recall the smile on His face,
As those words just rolled out
Like a fine red velvet carpet reserved –
For Royalty!
And what a sight to see,
Jesus was smiling but alas,
A tear slid down his cheek as well –
"A tear of joy", the Lord told me,
"For True Love is a joy to give,
So give as I have given".
I will never forget as He got up to leave
He turned around, embraced me and one last thing
I remember that he said –
He said "Without love, all is dead."
Chilling words from the Lord
And to this day I have never forgotten
Nor will I ever! –
As I sit in the garden now alone,
I ponder His words in the stillness of my soul.

Dark Night of the Soul

Visions of black –
Haunt my every move!
I make my way upstream
Unable to see but to feel the cold and wet,
Falling down hard on me!
Here we go! –
The sickness that destroys
Even the smallest rays of hope
Has wrung the bell again!
Here am I, defenseless as a child
Afraid of the white flashing lightning
And clapping thunder
That always accompanies it.
Seasons of a brighter day
Have long since faded away
As light hues of gold
Have rusted into an ugly orange
That smells of evil
And cuts like a cleaver!
O' dark night of the soul! –
I banish you to the four corners
And curse the day you were born!
I tip toe past sleeping hellhounds,
Only to trip over the bell's cord,
To hear it ring yet again to alert
For a fresh kill that is me!
Running through the shadows,
Tripping over rocks and smashing into boulders
That seem to have been set in my path!
I cry out to God

For mercy and protection! –
In Hell on Earth again
And the value of this life just keeps going down
Till light exists for me no more!
I am down for the count
In endless corridors of horror,
Filled with demons of the filthiest kind
And not one ounce out of my mind!
Reality smacks me raw
Until I am black and blue!–
But such is the path
That I must walk through!
Dark nights of the soul
Weigh on my heart so heavy
That it's all I can do to say,
"Yes Lord, I will make it another day"!

Fade Away

Flying through the shadows
Running through the night
I don't know what I'm doing
But I got to get it right, get it right!
Sunshine brightens even the darkest of stains
I'm doing spring cleaning, yeah
Re-arranging my brain!
O' the madness that is you!
What you try to understand
Is lost in the wind, lost in the wind!
I wonder where shall I begin –
So I can let you know,
Try to make you understand
That you must understand
Who I am, Where I came from, Where I am going,
So you can come too!
I want to spend it all with you, with you!
I try to tell you but you miss the catch
It's like you don't want to hear
What I need to let loose!
It's flying in the wind again
As I begin and begin and begin,
Is it just a lost cause?
I wonder as I fly through the nights
Taking to great heights,
To get to you, got to get to you!
Running in the shadows it seems,
Or is all this just a dream within a dream?
You stare blank as I hold my head,
Then I begin to wonder if you've even
heard a word I've said!
But it's all daisies and roses anyway,

What does it matter if all is lost from the past?
I can live with that, live with that!
Just hope it doesn't come into the light with me!
I'm just running through the night.
If that's okay, if that's alright!
I am done with the run! –
Can't catch me now,
Not even in your web.
Rainbow spreading wide,
The night visions have all died!
Resting in your arms,
Finding solace in your sweet embrace,
All my bad memories I will erase!
I will never ever speak of them again,
Pushing forward towards the mark,
The light is on even when the night is dark!
Illumination shakes me wildly,
As I dance in a trance before your eyes –
I won't ever comprise!
Who I am:
I will never hide!
Ah, Love, take me on a ride again –
Straight into your blue eyes!
Bring me sunshine, bring me rain,
We'll weather understanding together
And walk in between the pain! –
Of the thorns that are on the newly budding rose bushes,
In my soul and yours!
I am yours, I am yours!
And so, it goes, it goes,
On and on and on!
Let's begin anew! –
I won't try to be understood,
Just try to understand you, you!
It's all I can do, can do!
Cause I love you, love!

Goodbye night, hello day,
I was older when I started,
I am younger now today!
Fade away, fade away,
Fade away, fade away!

Heaven

Lend me the ocean! –
Salty in taste and smooth in touch
So that I may bathe and wash myself –
Pure and refined!
Bring me gold from the sky –
So with honey-dripped sunbeams
Falling down from Heaven –
I may dry myself shiny and new!
I dress myself in pink,
Dogwood's velvety petals
Slippery and silky in matter
As they form a small hurricane around me,
Caught up in gusts of whispering winds,
I am dressed like a Queen!
I drink from the nectar of the sweet and dear honeysuckle
As I find solace in the embrace of a fine young willow tree
That swoops down to gently lift me in its tender mercies!
I cry out softly to the neighboring birds,
with a quiet shout I say –
"Heaven, Heaven!"
and retire ever so peacefully
Into nature's illustrious song!

Heavenly Visitors

Rays of white hope fall down,
Each unique and glimmering
With their own twists and turns!
Winds from the north
Scatter them to the four corners
Of my yard as I think to myself,
Snowflakes must be the most
Beautiful and selfless creatures of all!
Filling up my frozen and barren yard
Like cottony clouds that used to live above
They ask for nothing and as they give, give, give –
Their ethereal brand of love!
Ah to watch them fall down on us all
Ushering in the Christmas spirit
Like ghosts from Christmas' past
And I think to myself,
Winter has visited us at last!
Such intense illumination
As they light up my yard
Lifting my soul to higher ground
And my Spirit set up for weeks on high
Gifts from Heaven
Treasures from above
All wrapped up in neat little packages
Full of God's good love!
After much absorption of this mesmerizing scene,
I return to my bed
And of snowflakes do dream!
Alas, Winter does take it all away
But God gives back such beauty in its quiet display!
It makes you wonder even in slumber
The Glorious Majesty of our Lord!

I Dream…

I dream of tall pine trees swaying in Fall's breeze
Roses drenched in yellow and red
Honeysuckles sweet to the taste
Green grasses high
Winter's warning whistle
Dancing rainbow leaves
Red cardinal gliding on the air
The earth swallowing up the orange sun
Moonbeams that streak the sky with lightning white
and star speckled lighthouses that liven up the night!
I dream of union with nature
Running and jumping into the scene
Making no sound – just listening and watching,
As if to catch a peek
Of nature wild –
Untamed by man's touch!
Yes, I dream!

I Thank You Lord

Sun as it sets, hits the pond
With a dazzling diamond effect
And I thank you Lord!
Flowers in bloom
Fills the breeze sweet and lifts my heavy soul
And I thank you Lord!
The beach at night with the moon brilliantly bright
And stars speckled upon a navy quilt dream
And I thank you Lord!
The trees in the fall, like a million rainbows glistening,
I stare in awe! –
And I thank you Lord!
The sun with its rays
Shines on birds as they play,
And I thank you Lord!
Walking in freshly fallen snow that shimmers and glows
Sends me into another world of peace
Filled with endless hopes and possibilities
And I thank you Lord!
These seasons, these miraculous sights
Are all lodged into my heart and mind's eye
And I am so grateful to have them help me get by,
And I, I thank you Lord!

I Will Overcome

I pray for rainstorms
To wash away my stains!
The darkness comes from the outside –
Not always from the inside
And like chimney soot settles on me!
So I pray for rainstorms
For Purity from this spirit-crushing world
And place my Spirit in a safe box
No longer free but safe! –
For I am a warrior! –
Green and blue war paint streaked over my face
Salty earth beneath my feet
Lines on my face from every battle won and lost!
I must protect my precious Spirit from you!
You cannot shake it, you cannot break it! –
Yet somehow you crush it anyway!
Still, I am an unflinching warrior
I feel no pain, only the sound of the crush!
Porcelain Spirit, I will protect you from the dark eyes
From the soot that settles fiercely and unconditionally
I will cut out with my blade all the darkness that binds
And throw it back into the center of
the earth where hell abides!
I pray for rainstorms and carry on, outer scars plenty,
I carry on, I carry on with eyes lit with flames!
I burn down glares and stares until they are but soot
That the rainstorms wash away!
I am too fast anyway and my Spirit grows stronger –
With each battle faced, to conquer
so as not to be conquered!
I carry on and pray for rainstorms
and feel the purity in each precious drop!

Soothing rain washes clean the cuts,
Sets my sights a glowing
Cause there is no way of knowing
when the next battle will be!
You can see my soul in my brown eyes as I am telltale!
Can you see the heart that beats with
its perfect rhythm lying within?
I am a warrior in this vicious spiritual battle we are engaged in!
I will not be conquered, soot covered, or cut anymore!
I will consume you will the white of my soul
that protrudes from my inner being,
From the flames that light up my eyes you will be dust!
I promise you, I will overcome!

Insane

Burning with red- hot- coal desire,
My eyes lit with flames!–
I set my pen to ink
To write of the insane!
It's not an easy task to complete
And takes a careful muse
But dare I shrink from a complaint,
I will be of no use!
So my story begins and ends
Strung together with pills and swords
And I can barely utter a word
To tell of bloody battles waged –
On my mind, body, and soul!
Can you see them on my heart strings?
Deep cuts, deep and wide –
I try to hide for I am shy!
I keep to myself so nobody knows
At night I cry! –
For release from my malfunctioning brain!
Cause I know so many afflicted,
And I know too much of pain!
So if my words do offend,
I apologize in advance
For I do not mean to intrude
But I must take at least take a chance.
My story is 44 years long!
The pages are war torn!
Where to begin?
Where to end?
I don't know –
But I am tired of hiding!
Tired of being so shy!

Maybe meet me tomorrow?
I'll tell you secrets of my soul
And the visions I see with my heart.
The two are not exclusive –
Not so far apart.
For I know so much of beauty
As it does surround,
But I also know of ugly,
And I erase it as I go
So it will not be found!
I'm bleeding internally!
You will never tell
How my heart does swell
With tears from all the monsoons.
It's been one too many moons
And one too many dark nights of the soul
And I've got a lot of grays I'm told!
For I am young but I am old!
So at last I end, with a deep sigh…
Maybe I'm insane
Maybe you are too
But we're not alone
And the Lord will see us through!

Kaleidoscope of Being

Stained glass soul
Illuminated by sunshine
See my eyes glow!
Red, green, yellow, blue!
A kaleidoscope of entrancement,
I am and with it
A myriad of moods and emotions,
Of valley and peaks that require
No explanation!
A simple Child of God
With a red wheelbarrow
Pulling it along
Sometimes dragging it along.
Have I grown at all?
Faith oozes from my skin,
Hope - the kite in my soul,
Flies high and strong!
I begin to sing a new song –
The blues have past, now it's jazz,
Maybe tomorrow, rock…
One never knows,
How the show will go…
Cause we are all shows
Or did you not know?
Soundtrack of my life
O' sing me home again!

Land of Dreams

I live in the space of dreams
Made of fabric dripping with ethereal seams!
Where people's hopes and desires
Are lit up like raging Heavenly fires!
Angels fly to and fro
As dreams they bloom and hope's bestowed
Upon all the dreamers in God's vast land
Who dare to believe on the Son of Man!
Angels respond to faith released
The pure of hearts strong belief
That things hoped for will not be deferred
And instead stand on the Rock of God's Holy Word!
For the Lord is both faithful and true,
To deliver His Promises to those that do
Cling to their faith and plant their seeds
And feed on God's word and his decrees!
So here am I in the land of dreams,
Blessed beyond measure to watch the Divine Plan
And to take part in delivering miracles
To those that can believe on Jesus the Son of Man!

Love's Labor

Souls glowing shimmering with rhyme
Every night we gather
Out of space and out of time!
We carry the world's load of troubles
On our bended backs
And dance around the campfire
Singing phrases filled with fact!
In a spinning frenzy, we pray
With all our strength and heart
That God will save all through grace
For that is our share and part!
Each night we gather,
We feast on love's labor,
Laugh till we cry,
And then off like a brush fire each of us flies!
For we will be back again the next night
To gather again in song
And pray to God he makes all straight
And rights all our wrongs!
For we carry the world's problems
Up like incense before the King
As we chant and holler,
Hoot and yell and sing!
It's all we can do and what we must
For God so loves the world
All the while that we are dust!
So pray we do
Our joyous songs
Before God Almighty
And gain the strength to carry on
As we clutch our crosses tightly!

Each night is like a Holy display
As our souls are completely free.
At the end, each of us kneels down
And God Blesses us, you see!
For we have been chosen
Since generations past
As mighty prayer warriors
Interceding in the gap!
With great humility
Do we fulfill our vows?
And with great responsibility
Take our final bows.

Lucky

Down in a psychedelic valley
Back up in a dream like peak
Watching the sun take hold –
Ah, the sweet serenity I seek!
Mozart's on the piano
Kicking out some tunes
Monet's in the garden
Pastelling some radical blooms!
Ansel Adams is with his camera –
Catching the entire scene with each flick
While I am here with pen and paper
Thinking, what a crazy chick!
To have such brilliant company
That I summoned here with words
Leaves me breathless this morning
With my pen dancing in Divine accord!
Frost and Dickenson are in the parlor,
Chatting over crumpets and tea,
And all I can think of is –
How lucky to be me!
When I create my masterpiece
It will go as such:
That nothing is impossible
And nothing's out of touch!
Dust given into passion
Sheer mortals scribbling on Life's Divine page!
As Shakespeare once told me, I do believe
All the world is indeed a stage!
My five minutes have come and gone now
Yes, it is time for me to part
Taking with me glorious sounding melodies
Mind-blowing photography and art!

Nighttime Brigade

Eyes ablaze with flames! –
Night time covers the sleeping earth
And I am out on the prowl!
The darkness entices me
Calls my name and I answer
As with my particular transformation,
I ready myself with sword and badge
Of a higher calling!
My enemies are many –
I am Captain of the Night Brigade!
Forever bound to watch over
Sleeping children nestled in their beds
Dreaming their pure heart dreams!
I call out my troops
As legions of angels appear
As if out of a cloud of obscurity!
We roam the earth
Flying high and low
Chasing the devil's minions far below!
Many are slain and return to the center
Of the earth where Hell resides!
The moon keeps record of our victories!
For it is known, the Kingdom of Heaven
Is of a child's heart, and so
We remain on lookout until the sun peeks
Through night's veil!
With one signal,
All Angels return to higher realms
As I re-transform to wait for nighttime
To call my name again!

O' Me

Drums beat on into the night, in my soul
Rhythm and blues every time
As I sit and ponder religion,
Drink tea
And wonder
What on earth
Has happened
To the likes of me!
Swaying, I rise
Begin to twirl
Tea in hand
Lost in motion
Wait…
Guitar solo
And I am lost forever
In the high hitting notes
Playing on and on
Into the early morning
In my heart!
I recall the Egyptian secrets of the dead
And how they built armies for themselves
To protect them in the afterlife.
Thank the Lord I am alive and well
And spin off into eternity!
I tell myself, "You are taken care of
Jesus has got your back!"–
As the music erupts into a drum solo
And I am taken into the land
Of ghosts again!
Smoke from the fire rises
All consuming

And eats up my form
As I think about The Pyramids
And how my small tomb
Just won't do!
I make plans for an elaborate display
To mark my departure
But remember I am neither Egyptian nor Pharaoh
And groove to the new beat before me
That is playing now on in my Spirit!
I must be me, I think
And make plans for my pyramid anyway!
The drums soften and begin to dissipate –
As another evening has been laid to rest!
I retire quickly, dancing
To the new found music
In my head
And make my way off to bed!
As I bid the night goodbye,
I make a pyramid in the sand with my toe
And twist into my slumber!

Note to Self

Contentment breeds apathy!
Freedom is the ability to let the flower in your soul bloom!
Hunger for the things that feed your soul!
Thirst for the spiritual fruits that make you soar!
Forgive easily and quickly!
Be a student and a teacher!
Everybody is precious!
There is no war in humility!
You are the enemy!
You are the hero you need!
Hum all the time!
Read, write, maybe even rhyme!
Love, it's free, but priceless, and has a way
of returning home unexpectedly!
Go slow!
Pick flowers!
Dance in a rainstorm!
Love yourself!
Call on God - He is there and will answer!
Tell someone you love them!
Thank God!
Draw, sculpt, play!
Don't put off tomorrow what you can do today!
Smile as much as you can!
Laugh often!
Cry, it's healing!
Everything is a gift!
Life is very short so dive right in!
Never apologize for who you are!
Your true friends will find you!
Build a sand castle!
Be good to yourself!

Listen to your conscience, it's your guide!
Live your dreams now!
Dare to take chances every day!
All things come to an end!
Be kind!
Honor your mother and father!
Be a blessing to a child!
Think!
And, always remember that Love is the ultimate weapon!

Ode to Spring

Ah, Bring me Spring in a cup –
Daisies for the offering,
Roses for the sacrifice.
The cascading mountains of clouds
Tell their secrets to the universe!
As I spread my wings and dance on evening's breath!
O' to fly amongst the Heavenly lights
And to look downward on the lush, green carpets
Bordered with pink and yellow tulips!
Ah spring - you effervescent season of beauty and hope –
I find rest in your floral bosom and sleep lazily
As sweet lavender breezes sweep me straight
Into the heaven's again!

On a Snowy Eve

No stranger's steps do I spy
On newly fallen flake
For no one else goes here but I
As I tread so ever late!
The moon, it shivers in blue sky
Like a white rose ready to explode
As I make my way, walking stick in hand
Out into the freshly fallen snow!
The yellow stars blink as if to say –
"Why go you alone and in this late way?"
But how can I ever express my choking awe
Of winter's scene and chilling bough?
My bounty lies in my wide-eyed view
Of the electric white snow I travel through!
Still I try to soak it all into my soul and I write –
Winter's Kingdom indeed reigns supreme tonight!

Second Chance

Rainbows dance on treetops
As lava sunbeams fill the air
Fresh bouquet of roses blooming
And I haven't got a care!
I am coming back to life –
Springing forward with the season,
Winter is an afterthought
And I don't care about the reason!
Waving a cool goodbye to death
Fire shoots through my veins
There's a lightness to my step
As a passing sun shower takes the reigns!
A new beginning, a grand new start –
Thank God Spring and Winter are not so far apart!
I get a second chance
Every single year
That Winter melts to new found life
Hurrying in the New Year!
Joy now fills my soul
Light enters my eyes once more
Winter's gone and over
And I can't wait to see what Spring has in store!

The Song is Eternal

Melodic trance
Played out in musical notes
Taking the form of the rainbow
Of colors of every single different tree!
The breeze offers the harmony
Never missing a beat playing right along
With the eternal song!
The lead singer in nature's band!
Together, I trip into a world
Of vast musical creations
That collide with color
And send me reeling!–
With great feeling
Into endless wonder and inspiration!
I am forever awe struck at God's Good Creations!
Sweetly sung and kindly played
The Symphony is as grand as it is great
And all for little ole' me
To absorb and see!
I am totally high on this explosive display
It nearly blows my mind away!
I float on right through my day
And I can hear the lyrics as they say
"Glory, Glory to the King!"
As I retire into the kaleidoscope of song
That is eternal!

Certain Kind of Storm

There is a certain kind of storm
That comes from
The inside out
And leaves Nothing
In Return!
It's a specific type of crime –
This storm
That rips and roars
Through endless corridors
Of souls and torments
The strongest
Of hearts!
It sickens quickly
Leaves abruptly
Disturbs everyone
In the house
And pays no rent!
There is a certain kind of storm
Brewing on the streets today
Carving out niches in soulless folks!
Aging the young before their time!
And who shall stop it from its life?
"None", says I, "for it is the very reason people weep,
And never know the reasons why!"

White Orchids

I dream of White Orchids –
Sprinkled with stardust
Radiating with pulses of moon glow
And I, I think of God
And how he can really put on a show!
Angels pour the Holy Spirit on me
And I am off like a brush fire
Taken into the midst of early morning dew drops
Weighed out precisely and place ever so carefully
On white orchids tender waking petals!
As the moon rescinds to but a speck in the sky
I see God's craftsmanship in the rising fire
Consuming the earth with its illuminating
Red and orange hues of grandeur!
Ah, I dream of White Orchids –
Sparkling underneath enveloping sunbeams
Swaying in the endless moment
Giving off their sweet perfume
And I, I think of God and wonder
Does he dream of White Orchids like me?

Winter Wonderland Night

Dancing underneath flying snowflakes
I shake the cold and trip the ride
Straight on over into the other side
Where fairies dance a Cajun rhythm
And elves are making their illustrious brew!
All is quiet and I am eternally alone
In God's masterpiece of snowfall, I call my home!
Free styling down the damp streets
I fly and spin and twist and turn
Unique and bright I am a snowflake
Who lightens up the night!
With howls and whispers of dreams untold,
I share my secrets with the blinking yellow stars
And leave footprints that are quickly covered
But the sun is near and the moon it falls
Just another night out there on the prowl!
I make my way back down the cobblestones
Into my bed, back into my zone!
A most excellent journey has come full round
I leave the other side just as it was found!
My whispers and howls turn into wind
And all my secrets have melted away
I lay my heavy head down on my goose down
Sun rises as the evening moon must turn and bow to day!
Waving goodbye to my friends who took a rest
A Winter Wonderland night is always the best!

Cathedral in My Heart

There's a Cathedral in my heart
And hymns emanating henceforth
There's clapping and singing
And plenty of good report!
The Choir is full of the Holy Ghost on high
As angels are sighted
Pleased as they pass by!
The Church members all groove in a Holy Ghost dance
And shout Hallelujah
Whenever they get the chance!
James Cleveland is present
As is Joyce Meyer
While incense is burned in a Heavenly frenzy desire!
It comes from within the souls
Pours out through the skin
Sent straight up to Heaven
We just can't keep it in!
There's shouting and praising
And speaking in tongues
There's stomping and dancing
A true charismatic service well done!
It occurs every Sunday
You're welcome to come
This Cathedral is open
To each and every one!

Off the Beaten Path

I don't want to fit in!
I don't want to conform!
So, I shall make a new path:
I shall walk by the light of the sun!
I shall lead by the glow of the moon!
With walking stick in hand
I shall make my own stand!
I'll let others go their way.
They run too fast anyway
Leaving nature untouched!
But I, I shall walk on wet leaves
I shall dance in rainstorms
I shall tip my hat to pink lightening –
Electricity tearing up the night!
I shall wear leather sandals
In whatever shall befall
I shall wear bright colors
And chase after the multi-colored leaves
I find in Fall!
I shall dance with snowflakes
I shall drip with rain
And deep inside I know
That this will keep me sane!
For to follow down the trampled path
Is not in the cards for me
As I merge with nature's song
It's all I can hear and see!
I've got a call to the wild
And I dare not miss what waits
My destiny ahead of me
Straight to Heaven's gates!
I will live in a small cottage

I will live off the land
I will write poems with raindrops
I will draw pictures in the sand!
I will not conform to the world
I will keep my individuality
And all the sights I see
Will indeed be between God and me!
For I am a traveling woman
Who has set her sights
On Heaven on Earth!
And it is all around us
Priceless in its worth!
The rats will have run their race
But I have pictures to take
In my heart, mind, and soul
Don't know where I am going
But I know the road will show!
So I take little with me
And under Pines I rest
God's good creations
Ah what a noble quest!

Revival

The wintry blues have long since passed.
Springtime revival is here at last!
Deep, deep within my soul
The music starts to take control!
As James Cleveland takes to the stage singing
"I claim a Victory at last"
The blues are sent far below!
Casting Crowns blows my heart away
With every single thing they play
With every single word they say
And Sonic Flood sings "Everyday"
And then onto Jars of Clay who sing
"Love can heal the broken
Hope can make you see…"
And all the while I'm clapping hands
And dancing and singing good and free!
Next, Third Day takes the stage together with Mercy Me
And as I've got new blood pumping through my veins,
Lifehouse steps up and does a set just for me!
Their "Hanging by a Moment"
Sets my soul on fire
As this Christian Concert Revival takes me even higher!
All come back on stage to collaborate on Amazing Grace
And words just can't describe the grateful tears
Rolling down my face!
I bow to Jesus, the Holy King
Who I give the Glory for the entire thing!
My blues have long since been replaced
By this Christian Revival deep within my soul
And I am back in rare form
After this amazing and incredible show!

Small Town Blues

I want to ride on wild horses!
I want to live in the sun's glorious hues!
I want to swallow up the ocean!
I want to sing away my blues!
Cause I have this beat in my soul
And it's starting to take control
I must fly away or die
I must try and not comply
With the rules of society!
For I am free in my soul
My heart has wings and needs to go!
I need to walk fast then slow!
To catch a glimpse of nature's scene!
I've got a machete to make my path!
And I've got just energy enough
To be just like a flash!
Where I am going I don't know
Tired of living in this town of broken dreams!
I've got aces up my sleeves
Yes, I am ready to play
Lay your cards down on the table
Just know I got the winning hand okay?
I want to slide down rainbows!
I want to bask in the rain!
I want to wake up with morning's dew!
Got to leave this small town game!
This town has too many rules
There stealing my smiles
And giving me the blues!
Time to tuck and roll out of this hole
And keep on keeping on!

Time to create a new song
Yes, you too can tag along!
We'll go together and leave at dusk
Before it's too late and this town makes us rust!
Cause I got the small town blues
And nothing to lose
We'll bust out of here and live on our dreams
Cause faith is the substance of things hoped yet unseen!
God's got a plan for us
We'll make it for sure
If there's one thing I know that I know
You've got to first open the door to what lays in store!
So, meet me tomorrow at the lakeside ready to go
I'll be there by nightfall and we'll bust out of this hole!
Goodbye small town and hello world
Tomorrow really means forever and I always keep my word!
We'll take to the highway and never leave a trace
There's so much more to life than this small town taste!
Living for God with all our might
If you have to live you might as well do it right!
As night falls down hard on my small town
I can't help but sigh
I told you, Lord I'm coming
For this town just makes me cry.
Going to fly on wings like eagles!
Going to run and never look back!
Going to keep my eye on Jesus!
Jesus is going to keep us right on track!

The Mystery of the Purple Violets

In the garden of my soul
Sweet purple violets grow!
In the conscience of my spirit
They whisper mysteries and I can hear it!
As Monarch butterflies,
Touched with orange powder Divine
Fly to and fro and on the purple violets do bestow
The gift of Life so grand!
Surely, I ponder this was planned
And done out of Love by God's Divine hand!
And in my heart of hearts
Where Jesus my King does reign
He tells me of the mysteries of the purple violets
And with a quiet small voice does explain
That they grow in times of inward rain.
I begin to collect them for I too
Have been touched by the Monarch's orange hue!
And rise up no longer down in times of soulful pain
For now, I know what the purple violets do!
They bring me joy to see me through!
What mysteries unfold when one grieves!
What beauty does the soul indeed leave!
When fettered by Grace and Love from the King
Oh, purple violets you make my heart sing!
And I was told by the Lord himself
That each of us has a garden in our soul
And during times when life gets tough
Flowers bloom within us all!
To this I bow my head in thanks
And give all Glory to my Lord

Who wrought out of pain such a beautiful thing
And left my soul humming in Divine accord!

Darkness Gone

Forever climbing up ladders!
Trying desperately to reach the light!
Running from the shadows!
Alive in the night!
What went wrong?
What went right?
Light shattered the darkness!
Removed me from the permanent night!
Now I'm sliding down rainbows
Bathing in rain showers
Smashing the hourglass
For Freedom is power!
Thought my dreams were dead!
Laid out as I mourned and wept
But the Lord had other plans for me
The way got narrow but not steep!
Grateful to the Lord!
I smile the ride Shake the many hands
In his presence I now abide!
Back to normal!
My chains are broken and off!
The circle dance is done!
My soul went from hard to soft!
Miracle has come on time!
Bluebird delivers the news!
I arise and walk and go
As sweet melodies overtake the blues!
In the backdrop of my life –
What went wrong?
What went right?
What a perilous and magnificent journey
From the darkness out into the light!

I Will Not Forget

"Hold on tight", I said
"The manic-depressive ride"
Brilliance and Madness
Oh the collision as stars collide!
I have been so low
Had to raise up my head to see
Drops of light
Fall down onto the likes of me!
Creature of the moon!
Now dancer of the sun!
The Lord has completed a task!
The ride back to normal is done!
Shaking off the dust
Drying off the sweat
I look around as if to see for the first time
I said, "Lord, all mine?"
Health is priceless and how I prayed
Dragged my body along for this day
Spirit willing but flesh is weak
Even my Spirit got bruised and burnt
On my many darkened adventures!
Bloody murderer O', devil I stomp you under my feet!
You cannot kill me, steal anything from me, or destroy me anymore
I will not forget what my eyes have seen!
Nor what my ears have heard!
I will not forget the others still left in the bitter darkness!
The ones who tenderly waited with me!
I will not forget!
No, I will definitely not forget a thing!

January Blues

Got them mean old January Blues!
All's to win when you got nothing to lose!
Lost in the tumultuous currents of the riptide
With my heart down at my ankles, I'm lucky to be alive!
My souls all tangled up in sadness and grief!
Dear God, please send some Divine relief!
Thoughts all twisted and vision is fuzzy and unclear
Sweet Jesus, please lift me up and out of here!
With these January Blues no news is good news!
Falling hard and fading so very fast!
Seconds turn to hours with this dark die cast!
Twisting and turning out and into my skin
All I can say is, "January, here we go again"!
Missing in action I will be once again I fear
As all my emotions battle for release into one single tear!
That glides down my cheek and onto the floor
I tell you Sweet Lord, I can't take it anymore!
The lightness of Spirit has up and gone
As joy and happiness are fleeting it seems
Does anybody else know what I mean?
When light fades so fast it seems that my destiny is cast!
How can a troubled soul in this dark land expect to last?
Dark colors paint their forms on my wall!
Shadows of the darkness begin to crawl!
Up and down and all around!
I've got to get to higher ground!
Lord, I'm standing on your promise that you'll see me through!
Cause these January Blues are killing me too!
Slow death that has no end in sight!
Ah the supernatural torture of the soul - the devil's delight!

Still I hang on tooth and nail
And bang my cup on the bars of my jail
For Jesus to come and set me free!
Man, oh man, these January Blues just won't let me be!
Can I get a witness here?
Is there anybody else out there?
Thick black night corrodes my soul!
Oh sweet Lord, just another dark night of the soul!

Picasso, Van Gogh, and I

Riding on the edge of the wind,
I am out with Pablo Picasso again!
Van Gogh was feeling rather low,
So we left him at home to mellow!
Taking nothing but red wine
We feast off sites of the Divine!
Sailing past the stratosphere
Our aim is up and out of here!
We've come to glimpse at least in part
God's masterpiece so much better than art!
And to gain some Heavenly inspiration
For we are born of artistic dedication!
Sailing through the galaxy we spy starbursts
That bloom and never seem to fade
In bright vivid colors of yellow and blue
As we hover in awe like two emblazed!
Gazing around as if in a trance,
We see two comets set forth as if in a dance!
And revel and revel till reveling can be no more
Wondering what else this blessed night has in store!
Just to see the Glorious Universe in part
Is enough to inspire Picasso's Art!
Or so he tells me - like he said –
"Without Godly inspiration, We might as well be dead".
But who can take their eyes off of earth?
So blue and so green and the sun's continual rebirth!
Passing Saturn's rings and catching a shot at Jupiter's spot
We sip red wine and argue a lot;
Old pals just having some fun
Till we realize Van Gogh must be done.
For though we took liberties ship and it brought us far

Van Gogh took to painting the nighttime stars!
Wanting more but missing our friend
We set sail back to earth again!
When we arrived we gave him some wine.
Van Gogh seemed rather lighter as if a burden
Had been declined!
We raced out to the yard to see what he had done
Picasso got there first and was left awestruck and dumb!
For while we were on our flight
Van Gogh was busy painting a starry night!
And though we had seen parts of God's masterpiece grand
Van Gogh had been touched by the Grace of God's hand!
We patted our friend and gave him three cheers!
For who would have known what would appear!
Picasso and I had soared with eagle's wings!
While Van Gogh had made his canvas sing!
Parting for another night
For it was very late
Picasso and I kissed and said goodbye
While Van Gogh was in a happier state!
So that is how my night went!
And how it went so fast!
Picasso and I stormed the Heavens!
And Van Gogh found peace at last!

Jesus

There's a song in my soul!
There's a passion that never dies!
It's to stare into the eyes of Truth!
The eyes of the One who never comprised!
There's a fever in my spirit!
There's a tap in my step!
Do you feel it – can you hear it?
With all due respect!
I am on the prowl for the Holy One
The One and Only Christ
The Absolute Truth – My heart's true delight!
I like to call him Jesus
And you may too
He's the Best Friend you could ask for
And then some I tell you!
If I could but find Jacob's ladder
I tell you no lie
I would ascend into the Third Heaven
Just to stare into Jesus's own eyes!
After that it would be over for me
And I would throw myself down
I would worship my Savior
While lying prostrate on the ground!
All that I ask for and all that I pray
Is that I get to do just that one fine glorious day!
To stare into such Holy eyes
That never sinned or compromised
To Finally know why I am
And gaze upon Beauty I could never afford
Will end my life-long search
And quench the passion for which I was birthed!

Lonely Still

I eat the Word!
I plant the Seeds of Faith!
I await the harvest!
With great expectation and Hope!
Still I miss you!
Incomplete am I without you!
You said you would never leave me nor forsake me!
But still I need your literal presence!
You are the piece I am waiting for –
Hoping for, dreaming for, expecting for,
And I am lonely still!
I have hoped for You before I knew what Hope was!
I have dreamt of you in visions grand!
And I await your call
For I am lonely still!
Surrounded by everything that is good and great
Kind Blessings that you provide me with
But still I am lonely without you!
I ache in my soul,
An ache that no one can heal but you!
Still you give me Beauty to comfort me
But I think you are the Beauty I am searching for –
With all my heart, soul, mind, and strength!
I know you are
And I am lonely still!
Who will cure this ache?
Wounded to the core I cry out to you
But you are not here
And I guess I will just have to wait
Till my turn comes!
Until then, I am lonely
Even with the beauty surrounding without you!

Soul Hungry

Spirit fed and led
I make my way through the swampland
Of my days without you!
I ache, I burn, I grieve!
Jesus have mercy on me!
There is a Revival in my soul
There is a Cathedral in my heart
Come, Jesus, Come!
You are the only piece that fits!
There is a hole in my soul!
Come and stand at the Pulpit!
Dance with me in the rain!
Hold me tight
Cause I can't do it tonight!
O' misery without you!
I cry thunderous storms
Filled with dark slicing lightning!
And groan unspeakable words!
Waiting on your return!
O' Friend, why hast thou forsaken me?
Just a stranger down here…
Lost without you…
Drowning in tear storms and sobs!
I think I shall die without you!
Don't you know you are the reason I am living?
I should be dead.
Don't you know I can't do it without you by my side?
"It's okay little one, for I too have cried.
But I need you here…
I am coming soon, hold tight"
The Lord replied!

Testimony

The flowers are blooming in my soul again!
The Purple Violets grow tall and wide!
Inward rain has fallen due to storm!
As I am taken to the foot of the cross
Where Jesus paid the final cost
For my freedom and salvation!
Eternal thanks and gratitude
Emanates from my fragile soul!
To the Lord who won it all
For little ole me…
And I am just dust
But I am loved by him
And I love him
With everything that I am!
Sanctus Real plays
"When I don't measure up to much in this life,
I'm a treasure in the arms of Christ!"
I am grooving and the Purple Violets are spreading like a brush fire
Across my once aching soul,
Which has finally found its rest in the Almighty!
I dance because I can't sit still!
I sing because I love too!
I shout because I want to be heard!
Jesus Christ has set me free!
And finally I am able to be me!
No more guilt or shame
New found freedom
Broke the bondages
Darkness receded –
A New Creation in the Lord, I am!

No longer in chains!
Hurray for the inward rain!
It sets the soul on fire!
And brings me closer to my God
My one true heart's desire!
Glory to God in the Highest
To Christ who made all things possible
Even for a speck of dust
Like little ole me!
This my friends is my testimony!

Thinking of You

Walking through a field,
Filled with perfectly yellow buttoned White Daises
The soft velvety petals hold on tight
As the winds blows them to and fro
Sliding through my delicate hands
I bend and pick one just for you!
It seemed a crime to disrupt the field
So serene and beautiful
And that's probably why
You drifted into my mind
On this picturesque afternoon.
As I walk alone in this Heavenly scene
I find a place to rest
Holding onto the daisy tenderly
I dream that one day
We'll be together forever, Lord.

A Day in the Life

I ride through a pile of words
On the back of an orange Monarch!
Putting the words together cohesively
To draw an image or conjure up a scent –
A soothing aroma to feast upon!
Blackbird flies in the azure sky like a speck
Of a whirlwind of flavor
While I sniff lilies by the pond
Dreaming away the day
On the back of an orange Monarch!
It's the only way to travel!
Magical sights that shake my being
As we coast on up into a cottony cloud formation
That never seems to end!
Bouncing from end to end in the City of Clouds!
Monarch lands to give life on a yellow daffodil
As I jump off give thanks for the ride
And wake into another dream!

Awake, Awake

We go about our days
With the Cheshire Moon smiling down upon us all
Not realizing we walk in a daze
Until something wakes us inside!
Sometimes it's all we can do not to breakdown in tears
As our hearts hang heavy leaking everywhere we go!
Or a wide eyed smile marks our faces
For something special is in the air that only we know!
The Cheshire moon keeps track of it all!
It makes no difference big or small!
When someone special has touched our hearts and gone
Or when past loved ones are remembered by such sad songs
These are the times that mark our lives
That call out our individual names
That leave us standing tall
Or feeling ever so small!
And I just wanted you to know
How I love you all so…
For my name has been called
My life has been marked
And I will never be the same
And I don't want to be…
So now I stand awake, at attention
And I pledge with tears
Never to fall asleep again.
The Cheshire moon makes its rounds
Recording all my sorrows and joys
As I cry out finally
"Awake, Awake" and stand tall!

Journey to Be Free

Traveling down alleyways giving way to waterfalls of colors
Which embrace me and transform me
From a mellow mood to one of illumination!
The devils stalks my every move
As I cling to God
And am washed clean by His blood!
Sacrifice with pain
For all the world to gain:
Soul Salvation!
Inner transformation
As I grieve the sins
And embrace Forgiveness!
I am renewed and refreshed!
Gliding on the wings of a blackbird
Sailing through the Heaven's grandeur
I see the sun as it sets in its remarkable purple goodbye!
I sit on the rocks at the beach and just cry
For the Love of God –
His Beauty is everywhere
But so few know why!
Riding on the crest of a wave
I make my way out deep in aqua waters
Sprinkled with rainbow fish
And slowly get lost into the embracing oceanic arms
Which envelop me in waves of love and peace!
Restoration of my soul!
I give up my control!
Rise and I am free!

Of Madness

It creeps up on you
When you are not looking!
The wild eyed ride
That takes you low and high
And the crashes in between
Leaving you wishing for immediate Salvation!
It steals, kills, and destroys
Like a violent tornado
Touching the ground of your very soul
And then leaving you there
Sobbing without control!
It's a battle most often fought internally.
Though the scars can be seen on the external,
Watch me on my mad ride
The tears that only God can count!
The bags under the eyes from a high ride
That leaves your body weary and edgy
The blank stare of a low
That only a few people do truly know!
To say I am crazy is much too easy and neat!
No, I am brilliant like a star shining
From a thousand miles away
In its beating yellow shine!
Yes I am the Cheshire moon smiling upon you
In its carved crescent smile
Watching down over you! –
Magnificent in its form and vibrancy!
I am the person working hard to keep up
Trying so hard to slow down
And all the while holding tight
Not to lose my grip!

O' Madness, what are you creating in me?
Your masterpiece?!
I am one of those who holds their head down in a low
Smiles at strangers in a high
And crashes deeply like the waves
At high tide down by the seaside!
I am something you will never understand!
Simply put I am me!
I am unique as you!
So please don't call me crazy,
Cause maybe, just maybe,
That is you!

Waiting

I write in the stillness of the night
To quiet the rumblings of my soul!
I seek to hear God
And I seek His beautiful face
As the rain tatters on the tin palette of my mind
And the morning birds begin their worship
I too begin mine!
All of nature is in a groan
For the Coming of the Son of Man
As we enter into the Time of Sorrows
It's only a matter of time
I tell my longing soul
Before you shall behold His Glory!
In every detail a perfect design
All the pieces fit
For the Lord is preparing His bride
And I groan too
For wanting more
But not lacking His presence!
I sense the urgency in the Spirit!
I heed the call –
To proclaim the Word to one and all!
The Lord says,
"I come as a thief in the night"
As I keep vigil
Candles burning bright!
Awaiting my True Love!
My True Life to begin
When Heaven and Earth collide
So shall come the Son of Man!

What a masterpiece I think as I wait
That the Lord created from a clean slate!
For all of nature is in a roar
As I set my sites on the green and blue hues
The rainbows, the tree frogs
The cool morning dew!
What glorious sights
Ah but none shall compare,
To the Coming of the Lord
I do await with great care!
Yes nature groans and roars
And inwardly I'm shaken
But in the stillness of the night
The Lord said," I will never leave you forsaken!"
Trust in the Lord I do with everything I am
I can't tell you anymore for I am waiting for the Son of Man!

Welcome and Goodbye

Welcome to the world!
Welcome to reality!
Speckled in rich diversity!
What I think and what I know
Is so little as the wild wind blows!
Forever a Child of God!
Forever learning
Reaching out and turning
As the buds start appearing on the trees
I can hear the Wisdom in the sweet breeze
As it sings to me
I can hear ancestors of old
I can hear the Lord's voice
I can hear it loud and bold!
"Come to me little child"
The wind it speaks to me,
"Come to me little child and I will set you free!"
I listen to the river talk as well
As I am now so much closer to Heaven
Then I used to be to Hell!
Oh, old sinner that I am
I want the White Robe
Into Heaven's gates one day go I
And walk forever in the sweet by and by!
"Come to me", says the wind,
Come and I go...
Out into the world
Full of brightness of color
And black and white still shots!
Ah life is grand
And I say, "Welcome to Transcendent Reality"

As the good Lord embraces me!
Life is sweet and life is good!
I welcome the world in!
Child at heart
Spiritual and light
Going to make it through alright!
Kaleidoscopes form in front of my eyes!
As I stare into the sun –
What a lovely surprise!
Birds sing their songs
I am grooving right along!
Won't someone come and play with me?
Come now I say and meet me in the sweet by and by!
Goodbye World!
Goodbye Reality!
I am off in the wind!
Lost eternally in divine immortality!

I Have…

I have written songs and lyrics
That swept like waves of madness
Over the black and white keys
As I violently played away –
For one must vent in one's own way!
I have stormed the gates of the gallows
And releasing all to their new found fate
Of freedom's touch!
I have remained strong for the cause –
For one must have a cause
Igniting passion's embrace!
I have soared the Heavens
On the back of a blackbird tasting
The breathtaking heartache of beauty
Created but solely for my aching eyes –
Even into the pang of the painfully beautiful!
I have fought a Thousand wars for love
And danced a Thousand victories
Over rainbows short and sweet
In country sides vast and wide –
For one must have purpose and Love is Life itself!
I have died a painful death over and over
And cried till my ribs they ached
Over life and what it takes from you!
Yet always giving back but never in the same form –
For one must allow themselves feeling!
I have travelled long distances in my heart
To places rich with treasures of the spiritual kind!
I have feasted upon banquets of kindness, humility, and hope!
Never to be turned away from the Lord's table –

For one must eat what is right to eat in the Lord's eyes!
I have lived through dark nights of the soul
That tore my innards to death and at the point of it
Found Jesus comforting and taking care of me!
And yes I am in love with my Maker!
For one must have True Love to really live!
A million climbs, a million falls
A million straightaways, a million walls
A million wounds, A million loves
A million thanks to the Lord above –
For one must know Jesus to truly be Free!

Shaken

Rainbow tears fall down
Onto my black canvas
Igniting it with power
That I had thought I had lost.
I dig deeper into my aching soul
And pull out gray musical notes
That transcend the speed of sound
And dance on air
With an aroma of lavender.
Even deeper I find
Surprisingly enough
That no I am not dead
Just a little shaken
From the fall!

Testimony II

I don't know what I've become –
I love the moon!
I love the sun!
I travel down beams
That glisten with gold
And for once in my life
My story has been told!
Spent over forty long years
In the wilderness
With the Lord
Now I am humming
In the Promised Land
In Total Divine Accord!
I'm so grateful to God My Gratitude
Spreads like thick roots
To the four corners of the earth!
For I have seen so much of the dark side
That it crushed me to the core
I clung to the Lord
But I had no idea what He had in store!
I grew up in pain
Pain so real my insides ached
Sometimes I even prayed for death
And for death did I wait!
Now I dance like David
Before the throne of God
The past has just faded into nothingness
And I am no longer sad!
Glory to God in the Highest
From one grateful soul
There was so much of Hell that I knew

Now I can speak of Heaven as well!
Life goes so fast
Gone in a second the darkness was...
Now in Heaven on Earth I do abide
So very thankful to be alive!
This is all the Good Lord's doing
And it's very sweet to the taste
Silky to the touch
And mesmerizing to my mind and soul!
Sorry Satan, I served my time!
Go back to Hell!
Thank you Jesus from the depth of my soul
All the Glory be to you, Lord!
I will never forget the price you paid for me to be well!

The Promised Land

Stepping into green pastures
That over flow with milk and honey
I taste the sweetness
Of the surrounding countryside!
Searching out God
I dance to the King of Kings!
To Jesus be the Glory Forever and Ever!
Not task to small
The Lord has kept His Promises to me!
Delivered and Healed
I am whole!
And I thank him so!
Happiness and Peace
Walk hand in hand
In my mind and soul!
Beyond satisfied I am!
Godly love flows
Freely through my belly
And I find
I cannot stop smiling
And Love for all has birthed in me!
Miracles abound
As I turn and turn
In love with everything!
Lost in darkness
Brought out into the Light
My heart bursts with Gratitude,
And Sheer Delight!
I see the Cross
Before my eyes
I can't help but shed –

Grateful tears
For this was one of the reasons
Our Lord died...
And Rose!
Grateful to the core
I just want more and more
Of Christ and less of me!
I had better get started –
The Faith Adventure
Begins now...
In the Promised Land!

Lost in Thought

Lost in thought
As the sun melts
Beyond the horizon
I think of how God's love
Never fails!
I think of friends
Old and new
And how blessed I am
To be able to
Say that I have been touched
By pure gems
Far too many times
For coincidence!
True Love requires a soft heart
With a gentle touch
And I feel I have been given so much!
I think of how God's love
Always triumphs in the end!
Ah love it makes one able to fly
Or the absence thereof to cry
But it is always worth the risk!

Under Construction

Temple of the Holy Spirit
Life of the Living God
Living and breathing inside of me!
Transforming me into Christ's likeness!
Every day I go from Happiness to Happiness
All for God's Great Glory do I give my life joyfully!
Transformation running deep
Tearing down strongholds
Building new spiritual cities in my soul!
I cry out for more for less of me is more of God!
I am constantly on the operating table!
Perfect Will of the Lord sails through the spiritual world
Into my broken and weak being reviving me every day!
My passion oozes from my mind and spirit and heart!
Ah to live from Glory to Glory all for Jesus!
This amen is my heart's delight!
I am under construction until the day I pass away!
God's Love is the carpet I wrap myself in
While all the surgeries are taking place!
And after all is done I go to be with the Son!
Until then reconstruction and deconstruction!
The Holy Spirit takes me
Reshapes me, and makes me
Less, until, I am no more!
For I am under construction!

The Way of the Pen

It's a tough road
A rough road
Left with only your pen, your paper
And a million memories!
The lingering scents
The unforgettable sights
What made it all wrong?!
What made it all right?!
Scribbling down notes
Fearing men in white coats!
The way of the pen
Is mysterious and fragile
Demanding the delicate surgery of mankind!
Words to entice
Words to be cruel
Words to be offensive
Words to make one seem a fool
Or the other route one may go
Words to be kind
Words to illuminate
Words to be shaken
Words so that no one is mistaken!
Such is the way of the pen!
It can make the mind bend!
It can bring tears or laughter
Pain or Joy!
It up to you
What will you employ?!
The way of the pen
It's up to you in the end!

www.ingramcontent.com/pod-product-compliance
Lightning Source LLC
Chambersburg PA
CBHW031231120626
46545CB00003B/1079